Fisherman's Wife

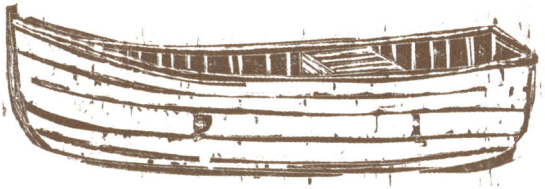

Fisherman's Wife

Josephine Lehman Thomas

Woodcuts by Julie Goldstein
Epilogue by Margaret Thomas Buchholz

DOWN THE SHORE
PUBLISHING
WEST CREEK, NEW JERSEY

Fisherman's Wife copyright © 2008 Margaret Thomas Buchholz. All rights reserved.
Illustrations copyright © 2008 Julie Goldstein. All rights reserved.

Material in this book may not be used, transmitted, uploaded or reproduced, in whole or in part in any form or by any means, digital, electronic or mechanical, including photocopying, video, audio or other recording, or by any information, storage and retrieval system without written permission, except in the case of brief quotations embodied in critical articles and reviews. For permissions or information, contact the publisher at the address below.

Box 100, West Creek, NJ 08092
www.down-the-shore.com

The words "Down The Shore" and the Down The Shore Publishing logos are registered U.S. Trademarks.
Manufactured in the United States.
10 9 8 7 6 5 4 3 2 1
First printing, 2008.
Book design by Leslee Ganss

Library of Congress Cataloging-in-Publication Data

Thomas, Josephine Lehman, d. 1959.
The fisherman's wife / Josephine Lehman Thomas ; illustrated by Julie Goldstein.
p. cm.
ISBN 978-1-59322-040-2
1. Thomas, Josephine Lehman, d. 1959--Miscellanea. 2. Authors, American--New Jersey--Miscellanea. 3. Fishers' spouses--New Jersey--Miscellanea. 4. Writing--Miscellanea. 5. New Jersey--Miscellanea. I. Title.
CT275.T55395A3 2008
809--dc22
2008013486

The wind off the Atlantic is raw at four o'clock in the morning, even in summer, and I pull my sweater closer about my throat as Tom and I walk down the sandy road between the tarpaper shacks where the fishermen live. The long, low fish shed on the dock and the high round shaft of Barnegat Lighthouse are beginning to take form out of the darkness. The slightly sour smell of Barnegat Bay salt marshes is strong in the air.

The waves lap softly against the fishing skiffs tied in orderly rows along the breakwater. The fishermen, awkward in rubber hip-boots and stiff yellow oilskins, shuffle clumsily past the piles of wooden boxes and wire baskets to stow their gear and tin lunch cans in their boats.

They make their preparations swiftly and with little to say beyond an occasional speculative comment about the weather.

"What you think about it, Axel?" The names one hears are like that — Axel and Olaf, Sven and Hans. Except for Tom and two or three native Barnegaters, these men of the fishing fleet are Scandinavians with the blood of seafaring Norsemen in their veins.

Axel scans the sky, the stars overhead, the faint pinkish glow on the eastern horizon. "Looks all right to me."

The other is getting the feel of the wind. "I don't think she shift before night."

Tom climbs down into his skiff and does something with a monkey wrench. There is a staccato sputter, and the motor starts with a roar. As it warms up, he pulls on oilskins and boots, and listens to the speculation about the weather. Axel, the acknowledged weather prophet, takes another long look at the sky.

"I think she is a good day. I shove off," he announces.

When one man starts the others follow. Tom kisses me good-bye, and Olaf Svenson in the

next boat looks embarrassed and nudges his partner. These Scandinavians would rather lose a day's catch of fish than be seen in a public gesture of affection toward their wives.

Lines are cast off, motors throttled down, and one by one the huge gray sea-skiffs slip out of the dock basin. Tom's boat leaves a scimitar of foam in its wake as it rounds a bend in the channel and disappears behind the low sand dunes, and I have my last glimpse of him as he stands at the tiller, fastening his oilskins more securely. It will be wet going through the narrow inlet where the tide is running swiftly out of Barnegat Bay and meeting the big rollers of the Atlantic.

The last boat is lost in the early morning grayness, and inside me is the dull emptiness I feel every time Tom puts to sea. I walk back down the road to where the flivver is parked, beside the little lunch room where two fish-truck drivers are going in for early morning coffee and fried potatoes. They glance at me curiously as I hurry along, and one asks the other a question. The answer comes to me clearly in the still morning air:

"Her? Oh, just one of the fishermen's wives."

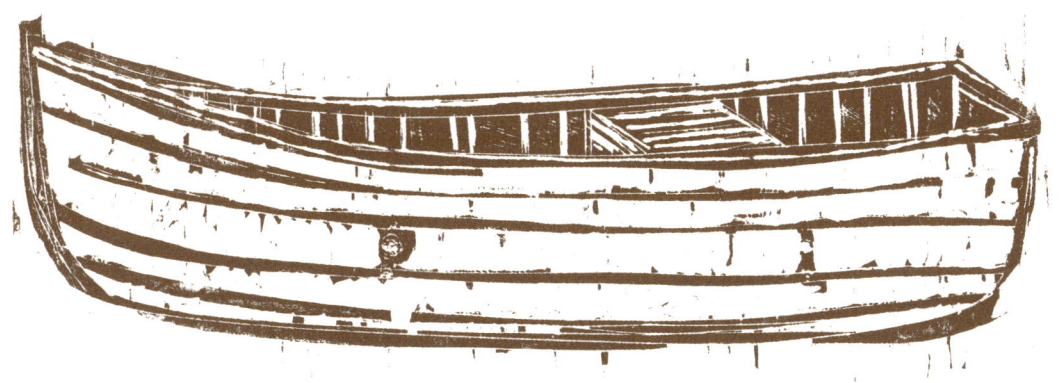

When Tom and I married, two years ago, my excellent journalistic salary, Tom's business, and the interest from his inherited securities gave us an income of almost a thousand dollars a month. Now we have not that much in a year. The business failed after being nursed through a year of steady losses. My salary ceased because of sickness and an ill-timed venture into freelancing. The income from our securities has shrunk two-thirds, chiefly because the aunt who bequeathed most of them to Tom had such unquestionable faith in South American bonds.

After months of forced idleness and fruitless search for a paying job, Tom had become sallow and thin, harassed by nervous indigestion and insomnia. To add to his worries, I

discovered I was going to have a baby. The beginning of summer found us with few tangible assets, not counting the kind known as frozen, except a quantity of furniture (and no place to put it), an expensive automobile we could not afford to use, and a motor boat acquired in the last year of our prosperity and still unfinished.

Tom had spent his summers since childhood on Barnegat Bay, and his boat was the same type of huge oceangoing skiff the Barnegat fishermen use. That boat was more than a hobby to him — it was practically a mistress, the recipient of secret extravagances, the occasion for numerous trips, ostensibly to "see a man in Philadelphia," which invariably were made by the roundabout and wholly illogical way of Barnegat. We couldn't afford to keep the car, but I knew Tom would rather pawn his clothes than sell the boat. He decided to convert it from an expensive plaything into a commercial investment, and join the fishing fleet.

The fishing village clusters around Barnegat Light on the long sliver of island that lies six miles off the New Jersey shore between Barnegat Bay and the Atlantic. A mile or so down the road we found a scantily furnished cottage for twenty-five dollars a month, where one cooked

and ate and lived and entertained in the same room. I did things to its glaring whitewashed walls with blue and red chintz, while Tom worked from dawn to dark fitting the skiff with what his optimistic nature considered the minimum of necessary equipment.

When the boat was being built, we pored over plans for trim-lined cabins and gay awninged cockpits where one served tall cold drinks in nautically monogrammed sea-going china and crystal. We made long lists of bronze and chromium fittings, chronometers, shining binnacles — all the enticing gadgets the more expensive yachting magazines advertise. Before we could buy them the money was gone, and instead of a smart cabin cruiser, we owned an open twenty-six-footer with no equipment except the powerful motor. Tom added fishing gear, three soggy life preservers, a home-made anchor, and a second-hand compass always at least four points off. He hired a native Barnegater as fishing partner, paid thirty dollars for a ten-year-old Model T flivver to provide transportation between house and dock, and in a week was ready to go to sea.

𝓐 deep sea fisherman's day begins at a quarter past three. There is no sign of dawn when we are wrenched awake by the strident alarm clock. Half asleep, I fumble for slippers and warm bathrobe. (The peach satin negligee that cost more than the flivver is packed away in New York.) I awake by degrees as I go through the routine of breakfast. Coffee on one burner of the smoky oil

stove; water for the eggs on the other. The pounding of the surf sounds ominously loud to me. As I dash cold water on my face at the kitchen sink, I am thinking about the treacherous bar at the inlet. I squeeze the oranges, fetch cream and bread and marmalade from the little icebox, and dress in snatches — woolen slacks, jumper and sneakers, a comb through my hair. Thank God I had that permanent. There is no time to put on powder or lipstick. My face looks pinched and old to me, and I hope Tom is too sleepy to notice.

    The stove will not burn, and the first waves of early morning nausea make me short-tempered. "Damn it, darling, will you *please* not take my stove matches away." Tom says he is sorry, and I am ashamed. He is never irritable before breakfast or any other time.

    He eats while I pack his lunch in a tin biscuit can. The four sandwiches. Two apples. The slab of chocolate cake. A bottle of lemonade. While he goes out to crank the flivver, I manage a few swallows of orange juice, but my stomach revolts at coffee. I put on an extra sweater and ride with him to the dock to bring back the car.

    If I am too ill, or do not want the car during the day, Tom goes alone. I stand at the window and watch the red rear light of the flivver until it is lost around a curve. A fish truck returning from a night trip to Philadelphia rumbles past and disappears, its clatter drowned by the boom of the surf. Then there is nothing but the dark empty road and the thundering Atlantic. "Please God, don't let the bar be too rough," I pray, as I prayed for things when I was a child. I put the butter and cream into the icebox and try to go back to sleep. The bed seems wide and empty. In the east are the first flaming streaks of dawn.

S lowly and laboriously,
I grew accustomed to the
new routine. For two months I was
wretched and ill most of each day, and given to morbid brooding over our
poverty. In my heart I knew that Tom's smile and the way he writes "JoDear" as
one word meant more to me than all the money in the world — but as I dragged
miserably through the morning housework, every domestic task seemed laden
with reminders of another life. Washing the blue and red breakfast dishes brought
back memories of Prague and the day my Vienna-bound plane was halted there
by fog. Ironing my best embroidered napkins and table runners, I saw the crooked
sun-drenched street in Rome where I paid three times too much for them. And

 25

emptying the ash trays with the crossed-sabre trademark invoked a gay picture of the January day I bought them in Dresden — afternoon coffee and *belegtes brotchen* at a table overlooking the ice cakes floating down the Elbe, the orchestra playing the latest seductive tango. All that was another existence, and that young woman was someone else, someone whose confident plans for the future had nothing to do with being a fisherman's wife on a barren island off the Jersey coast.

 Lunch and a cup of hot tea usually induced a more cheerful mood. In the afternoons I walked far up the beach to lie in the sun on the hard white sand, alone except for a steamer crawling along the horizon, the gulls wheeling overhead, and the flocks of solemn little sandpipers, wholly absorbed in their own pursuits, running stiff-legged over the sand. I spent long drowsy hours there by the dunes, content to listen to the sound of the surf, captivated by the changing moods of the sea, until I grew to understand the lure it has for Tom, to comprehend how one can both love and hate it as one loves and hates a mistress who holds him in her spell.

 One day is much like another. By four o'clock I begin to look for Tom. I go back to the cottage, prepare vegetables, try to read. By six o'clock I know he will be there any moment, and I put the potatoes and dessert into the oven. Forty minutes later I turn down the fire to retard the cooking, and sit at the window watching the automobiles coming around the bend in the road. By eight o'clock my imagination has encompassed every possible calamity that could beset him.

I remember the two Norwegians, veteran fishermen for twenty years, who were lost when their skiff capsized on the bar last year. I think about the bad heart Tom has had ever since Belleau Wood. It begins to rain, and I go down to the beach to see if the surf is heavier. By nine o'clock I am numb and choked from worrying, and when at last Tom strides in, ruddy and glowing from the rain and preceded by a strong odor of fish, I cry weakly down his neck and search futilely for my handkerchief. He offers me his own, one of his best monogrammed ones, which has evidently been used to clean out the fish bin.

"Never mind, honey, let 'em drip. You can't make me any wetter. I'm sorry I'm so late, Jo. We had a swell catch and I didn't want to leave."

I light the stove again and bring his dressing gown and slippers while he peels off his wet clothes and drops them out of the window to air.

"My God, I'm hungry. Is that Brown Betty I smell? Come back here; you get another kiss. Look, JoDear, do I have to wash all over first?"

The fishy odor he exudes makes me deathly sick, but I compromise. "All right, just your hands and face then, and finish afterward." I hurry to put the food on the table. "You shouldn't go so long without eating. It must be ten hours."

"Thirteen."

"Thirteen what?"

"Thirteen hours since food." His voice is indistinct from baked potato and omelet. "I got hungry as a bear at nine o'clock this morning and polished off my lunch."

"Oh, Tom, all of it?"

"Well, no, but I gave the rest to Bill. He didn't have any breakfast."

Bill is another fisherman — a tall young Finlander, hair unbelievably yellow, shoulders unbelievably broad, and the coat of arms of Finland tattooed in violent blue on his powerful forearms. Tom brought him home to lunch one day. He speaks English slowly and carefully and pleasantly, but was ill at ease and inarticulate at first, and had to be urged to eat. He was puzzled by the cold jellied-beef consomme, and embarrassed by the extra spoon and the napkin. Both Tom and I liked him immensely.

Bill came often after his first shyness had gone. On rainy days he and Tom burrowed into our collection of yachting magazines and marine catalogs, and spent hours discussing trawling and squidding, self-bailing hulls, clinker construction, and other subjects unintelligible to me. Bill could not understand anyone's being afraid of the sea, as I was, and despite warning glances and surreptitious kicks from Tom he innocently divulged in his conversation all the nautical mishaps my well-meaning husband tried to conceal from me: Tom's rudder unshipped by a heavy following sea on the bar, the dead engine twenty miles at sea and the four-hour wait until a Coast Guard cutter saw his distress signal (his pale blue B.V.D.'s flying aloft), the number of times he went out without a compass or life preservers. Tom will never learn to take life preservers seriously.

 Tom was anxious for me to go on a fishing trip to convince me it was merely

a prosaic day's work. After waiting weeks, a day finally came when the weather report and my internal state were simultaneously favorable. We were off in the flivver together, through the daybreak scenes that had grown so familiar — the stunted cedars and silver-green bayberry bushes ghostly and shadowy on the white dunes, Barnegat Bay flat and calm to the west of the island, the pounding surf and rosy sky to the east, and the red and white buildings of the Coast Guard station with the charming name of Loveladies.

  We shoved off as soon as we reached the dock, rounded the end of the island under the long beams Barnegat Light threw far out to sea, and approached the bar. There was just enough daylight to see the buoys. Tom was at the tiller, and Jim, his fishing partner, stood at the motor controls to adjust the speed at Tom's orders to meet the incoming seas. The big skiff breasted them beautifully, and ten minutes later we were riding the long even swells of the Atlantic. The throttle was opened wider, and a compass course set for the ``ridge'' — the shallow banks twenty miles offshore where the schools of bluefish run. It takes more than an hour to reach there, and the fish bite best at daybreak.

We passed the lightship nine miles out at sea. Turning to say something to Tom, I discovered the shoreline had disappeared behind the horizon. We were out of sight of land, and the skiff seemed very small in the wide expanse of water. I was glad of the half dozen other fishing boats nearby.

"Are you all right, Jo?" Tom was shouting above the roar of the unmuffled engine.

"Fine," I lied, sucking surreptitiously at the lemon I had put in my sweater pocket. Tom smoked at the tiller, and Jim, lazily chewing tobacco, began cutting up moss bunker, the oily fish used as bait. They were moss bunker that had been dead a long time, and I moved to windward of them.

We sighted the high masts of the big sailing smacks that come down here from New York, and altered course toward them. After cruising around to see which of the other skiffs were "pulling," we selected a spot not far from Axel, who has an uncanny instinct for finding fish if fish are to be found. The engine was stopped, the anchor lowered, and Jim began "grinding," putting the moss bunker bait through what looked like an over-sized kitchen meat chopper attached to the starboard gunwale of the skiff. The nauseous mess that emerged was thrown overboard a handful at a time. The oil in it smoothed the water and made a slick on the surface. Then larger pieces of the bait were put on the two lines let over the stern into the slick. Tom attended to the lines and Jim to the grinder. We waited five minutes, ten. I was eager and impatient, and anxious to help. Another five minutes. There was a flash of brilliant blue just under the surface, then another and another. The water became radiant with streaks of bright color. We had found a big school of bluefish. They were attracted by the slick, and darted greedily at the largest particles of bait in the water — the ones with the hooks inside.

The fish bit as fast as they could be pulled in and unhooked. Tom put on a pair of old leather gloves to protect his fingers from the wet lines and also from possible bites from vindictive victims. All about us, other boats were pulling in fully as many. The fish were biting so fast Tom could not attend to both lines, and I helped him bait the hooks, in my excitement and enthusiasm forgetting my distaste for the moss-bunkers. Even the stoical Scandinavians grow excited over a catch like this.

"Look at the size of this baby, Jo." I admired it and Tom tossed the big blue into the bin.

A six-pounder lunged off Jim's hook, and the lanky Barnegater spat a resentful stream of tobacco juice after it. "God damn, there goes fifty cents."

The fish bit steadily until the bin was more than half full. Then the flashes of blue in the water grew scarcer, and it was several minutes between bites. The three of us amused ourselves throwing bits of bait to the flocks of Mother Carey's chickens twittering over the water. Watching the little birds catch the tidbits in midair, I realized I was very hungry, although it was still long before noon. We opened the lunch tin and ate sandwiches ravenously out of unspeakably dirty hands.

The midday sun was warm, and after the last sandwich had disappeared I took off my heavy hip boots and yellow oilskins and stretched out forward for a nap. When I awoke, a half dozen more fish had been caught but none of the skiffs had repeated the luck of early morning. Toward five o'clock, one boat started for shore, and the others raised anchor and followed.

A stiff westerly breeze had come up. We began to ship water, and I put on my oilskins and boots again. The waves grew higher as we neared the bar. I was very tired by this time, and worried about going through the inlet. Tom showed no apprehension, but his remark that ``it's always worse coming back than going out'' did nothing to allay my fears. I started to go forward — because the life jackets were stowed in the bow.

``Stay back here,'' Tom called sharply from the tiller. He knew the bow must be light to help the skiff ride the seas and keep her from burying her nose as she slid down into the trough of the waves. I clutched the gunwale in unconcealed terror as sea after sea rose into high curling crests and crashed into churning foam around us. This was the place where the two Norwegians were drowned. In that pounding surf even a good swimmer would have little chance.

Then suddenly we were through, and rounding the lighthouse into the bay. Throttles were wide open as each boat tried to reach the dock first. There was the noise of the ice crushers as we nosed in and tied up. Heavy baskets of fish were swung lightly from boat to dock — not only bluefish, but flounder and weakfish and seabass, and squirming gray lobsters making futile slaps at their captors with their claws. The news of the big catch had been brought in by the first arrivals, and already trucks were backed up to the dockshed to load the fish and start the night drive to Philadelphia and New York.

The smell of fish and gasoline sickened me, and I walked down the road while Tom made fast the skiff. Around me the lobster pots and buoys were stacked everywhere, nets were stretched to dry, and boats lay pulled out to have their bottoms copper painted. I sat on an overturned lobster pot and listened to the sounds from the waterfront — broken clam shells crunching under foot as the fishermen hurried away to hot food and coffee, the chopping of ice, the thump of heavy boxes, the snorting trucks. The sound of the surf on the other side of the island was faint and dull. It was good to be on land again.

We brought in 1,100 pounds of fish in that catch, more than a half ton after they were gutted, but the wholesale price was only four cents a pound. After paying for ice and boxes, shipping and commissions, gasoline and oil and bait, and sharing the proceeds with his partner, there was less than ten dollars left for Tom for the day's work. And that was a good catch, one of the best of the season.

37

38

Often Tom did not make expenses. There were days when the bluefish could not be found, other days when they refused to bite for some reason known only to themselves. Or the sea was too choppy for fishing, and the end of a sixteen-hour working day would find Tom coming home exhausted and white and seasick, with nothing to show for seven dollars' worth of bait and gasoline except three small bluefish and a worthless young shark.

"And I used to do this for fun," he marvelled.

There were long stretches of squally weather, when no boats ventured outside the bay, and the fishermen overhauled their engines and mended their gear, talking of the old days, two or three years ago, when bluefish sold in Fulton Market for fifty cents a pound, and five-hundred-dollar catches were not unusual.

For three weeks Tom did not have a catch big enough to pay expenses, and there was one weekend when we had nothing to eat but boiled rice and apples. As a last resort, he offered himself and the skiff for hire, to take weekenders deep sea fishing. A party of Philadelphians engaged him every Sunday for six weeks, and were satisfied if they caught one bluefish apiece to uphold their piscatorial reputations. They paid Tom twenty dollars a trip, and once they brought him a gift of old clothes — a half dozen coats and trousers of the type known ten years ago as "cake eater." I was first amused, thinking of the excellently tailored suits hanging unused in Tom's wardrobe, then indignant.

"How could they? Can't they see you're different?"

"The only way I'm different is that I'm not half so good a fisherman as the Squareheads. I don't look any different, you know."

He was right. In disreputable dungarees or oilskins, face and hands smeared with grease and perspiration, all men look pretty much alike. Tom's hands were never wholly clean any more, and his nails defied the stoutest mechanic's soap. He grew careless about shaving, and had his hair cut only when the tendrils began to curl about his ears.

These things no longer seemed important to me. I was content that he was growing strong and brown again, that the whites of his eyes were white instead of yellow, that the box of bicarbonate of soda stood neglected on the kitchen shelf, and that he slept the sleep of healthy fatigue and grinned at me when I shook him awake.

 My own attacks of illness began to abate, and keeping house grew less laborious. The same grim satisfaction I once felt over scooping a rival foreign correspondent was now aroused by achieving a perfectly cooked meal, or ironing Tom's shirts without leaving a wrinkle in the collar. Doing my own washing and hanging clothes out on a line seemed a balder admission of poverty than any we had yet made, and at first I hung the wet things over an inadequate five-foot length of twine above the stove, where they remained damp for three days. After a month of this I said "what the Hell?" and put everything out to flap in the sun and wind and dry in two hours. After the first time, I didn't mind.

When the Sunday fishing party came no more with its weekly twenty dollars, I learned to practice economies I would have considered flatly impossible two years ago. I understood that the United States Army ration allows twelve cents a meal for food, but the best I could do was thirteen. Searching for sales on rice, butter, flour, and sugar, I dreamed of a shopping list that would again include mushrooms, Camembert cheese, sweetbreads — luxuries that are outlawed when every nickel is counted for staples.

By September I was reduced to my last pair of stockings, even though I had gone barelegged all summer. Three-dollar face powder and thirty-dollar French perfume were merely memories, and my toilet articles came from the five-and-ten.

We learned to take pleasure in simple things — our nightly extravagance of ice cream cones (the small five-cent ones) from the general store, an occasional movie, Tom being at home for a leisurely Sunday morning breakfast of waffles and both of us trying to get the *Times* book review first, the yellow-haired Bill bringing us a basket of succulent baby lobsters. They were "bootleg" lobsters, below the minimum legal size, but we asked no questions.

It was a gala day when Tom came home with a bunch of golden calendulas bought at a wayside stand on the mainland, for few flowers grow on this sandy island. Their tawny brightness recalled the talisman roses that played a persuasive role in his courtship.

"They only cost ten cents a dozen," he admitted. "I remembered you liked yellow."

The ten cents was the amount he allowed himself daily for the cheap cigarettes he had substituted for his favorite brand.

The months passed. The scrub cedars that cling precariously to the white dunes turned a duller green, the bayberry bushes grew brown, the summer bathers were gone, and the long white beach was left to the gulls and sandpipers. The wild ducks and geese began to fly south, and the sound of firing was heard all day from the shooting blinds in the marshes across the bay. Heavy autumn fogs hung over the island, and at night the hoarse uneasy rumble of the fog horns of passing steamers punctuated the boom of the surf.

One day there was an ominous sky, a long ground swell, and an uncertain wind that veered and shifted. The barometer fell steadily, and the surf pounded more heavily. In the afternoon Tom brought his boat from the fishing dock and anchored it in a cove of the bay near the cottage to have it within sight.

That night the first northeaster came howling out of the Atlantic. The cottage shook and quivered in the sharp gusts, and the rain dashed against the panes like handfuls of gravel. The electric current was off, and Tom stumbled about barefoot in the dark, closing windows, swearing fluently when he stepped on the sharp heels of my overturned bedroom slippers. In ten minutes he was asleep again, but I lay awake listening to the wind, and plagued by the vague worries and forebodings a pregnant woman has in the night. I knew this was the beginning of winter, and we had to plan what to do when we left the island — to face again the disheartening search for a job.

Tom heard me stirring and turning, and asked if I was all right. "I can't sleep either," he lied. "Let's play rummy."

He lighted a candle, wrapped my bathrobe around my shoulders, and dragged out a hatbox to put between us in bed for a card table. It was pleasant and intimate in the little circle of candlelight, with the cards clicking down on the gay pink and black stripes of the pasteboard hatbox. The box bore the name of a great establishment in the rue St. Honore, and the 900 francs I paid for the scrap of black felt it originally contained did not seem excessive then. I lunched in the Bois that day — but Paris is far away and long ago, and Tom beside me concealing his own weariness to help me through a wakeful night is very real.

    The gale raged through the night and the next day, shaking the little cottage until I feared it would be torn from its foundations. By mid-afternoon the sea was breaking over the bulkheads and through the dunes, and sweeping broken timbers as far as the post office. The high wind sent icy blasts through loose window sashes and under the doors, and I shivered in three sweaters as I stoked the little stove with driftwood.

    The second morning of the northeaster the tide was over the island and the cottage was surrounded by water. In hip-boots and oilskins we waded through it to the beach, shutting our eyes and lowering our heads against the sand that whirled off the tops of the dunes and cut into the skin like powdered glass. On the other side of the dunes everything was gray and white —

pale gray sky, lines of white breakers foaming to the horizon on the mountainous waves of a dark gray sea, white suds of spume and spindrift whirling over the sand. The rain lashed at our faces and the wind tore at our breath. Walking against it was like pushing a solid weight, and I made little more progress than the gulls that hovered almost motionless overhead as they tried to fly out to sea. The beach was deserted except for Tom and me and an occasional plucky little sandpiper.

  The northeaster blew itself out, calmer weather followed, and other storms came and went. The bluefish season ended, and the fishermen changed to cod-fishing gear, although by this time there were only a few days each month when it was safe for the fleet to venture far outside.

  Shut in together for days at a time by long stretches of stormy weather, I found it tragically easy to slump, physically and mentally, especially in the inertia natural to my condition. I had to force myself to put on a bright dress, to polish my nails and wave my hair, to cook Tom's favorite dishes, to manufacture foolish little surprises to stimulate and vivify the continual contact of marriage. Preserving an illusion of loveliness and romance is difficult when there is utter lack of privacy, when the only plumbing is at the kitchen sink, and icy draughts from outside make Spartan fortitude necessary for even the minimum of bathing. The ``jolly little coarsenesses of life'' are not always jolly.

  Nevertheless, we were happy. It was a satisfaction to Tom to know he was providing a living for us, even by manual labor, and some answering primitive instinct made me content to cook and tend the hearth and breed. We stayed on the island until two months before the child was born, and when we left, we left reluctantly. Besides health, this simple elemental life, in all its barrenness and frugality, had given us a deeper feeling of fulfillment in marriage, the common bond of each having worked hard for the other. Something much finer was welded between us than we found in the first prosperous days of our marriage, when our lives followed two distinct paths and we couldn't afford a baby.

Epilogue

Josephine's memories of the young woman who was "someone else," were of her own life as an editor and ghostwriter for Lowell Thomas, the legendary author and journalist who brought Gandhi and Lawrence of Arabia into the public consciousness. She worked for him during the 1920s, traveling back and forth across the Atlantic and throughout Europe and the Caribbean, interviewing the men who would be the subjects of his books.

The 1929 stock market crash did not affect her at first; although she lost all her savings, she kept her job. But she wanted to write a book and took a leave of absence for the summer of 1930 to get started. In a few months, however, she was "torn away" from the book by Thomas when he got a radio contract with CBS and she went to work as a news writer. Josephine said, "I tried to polish up my own book but it meant quicker money working for L.T. than for myself." At about the same time she met Reynold Thomas and, she wrote to an old friend, "That was my finish."

 My parents, Josephine and Reynold, were married with little fuss in March, 1931 at New York's City Hall. A year later, at age thirty-four, Jo was pregnant, and Reynold's family business succumbed to the Depression. She wrote, "I was too ill to even look at a typewriter. We came down to Long Beach Island where Reynold had spent his childhood summers, as it would benefit us both in health. Reynold was very thin and jumpy from business worries and for several months I could hardly hold my head up. He was gassed in the war and was told by doctors he must live an outside life if he wanted to keep fit."

 They had just enough investment income to live on, but as the dividends dried up and the Depression deepened they lived "slimmer and slimmer."

 "Reynold decided he could use his boat for commercial fishing," she wrote, "but by the end of the summer he was $300 poorer than if he had just put the boat in drydock and twiddled his fingers. But miraculously, he stopped having heart attacks for the first time in ten years."

 Jo finished *Fisherman's Wife*, then they returned to New York. She wrote her sister back in Michigan: "I am sending you a carbon of a story I did about life down at the shore. Being very personal, I changed a few details, but in the main it is true. The original is going the rounds of the editors."

She sold the article to *Scribner's* and it was published in their magazine in July 1933, three months after I was born. We settled in Harvey Cedars and the $500 she received sustained the little family for a year. Jo thought she could help support them by writing.

A second baby three years later and a diagnosis of breast cancer kept Josephine from realizing her dreams. She wrote, "Here I live, piling up the most marvelous material for writing, but it's almost impossible to find the time or strength to do it. I still write all the time in spirit, but I feel it's my job to raise my children at this age."

During World War II my father took a defense industry job at the Camden shipyards and my mother went back to the typewriter. Night after night my brother and I were lulled to sleep by pounding surf punctuated by the staccato of clacking keys; Jo had started a novel about two children who discover a cache of arms hidden in the dunes by German spies. To augment the family income she took on the unpopular job of tax collector for Harvey Cedars. Her former boss broadcast the news every evening at 6:45 and the dinner hour was arranged so my parents had coffee as he came on. We children were expected to pay attention. My mother tearfully tried to explain the difference between a German and a Nazi. She became depressed by the war news and turned to gardening. It was difficult to grow flowers in the sand, she said. I remember her digging furiously; moving plants here, then there, then back again. When I asked why she didn't just leave them in one place she said, "Because I can't afford a psychiatrist."

Life got better after the war, as business boomed. In 1950 a summer newspaper called *The Beachcomber* started and my mother hauled out her old Royal portable and wrote feature stories and garden and cooking columns. The cancer recurred and metastasized in 1952; doctors gave her two years to live. She suffered huge doses of radiation and was in and out of the hospital for several years, but struggled to maintain a normal life. She had more years than anticipated and in 1955, when I graduated from college, married and bought that newspaper, my mother turned in copy every week for three summers.

During the summer of 1959 she went back into the hospital for the last time and as I held my mother's hand shortly before she died, studying the strength, determination and intelligence in her face, I remembered she had once told me, "Even when I'm dying no one will believe me, I always look so damn healthy."

Margaret Thomas Buchholz
Harvey Cedars, NJ